The

BLOOMING

LOVE

Here it is!

ELIZABETH EDIONWE, M.ED.

Published by Reality of Life, Richmond, Texas

ISBN 978-1-7359115-6-4

Printed in the United States of America

CONTENTS

<u>LOVE</u>:

the only everlasting glue

"And you shall know the truth, and the truth shall set you free."

- John 8:32

INTRODUCTION

Welcome. Reader, it is not by chance you are reading this book today because the information here will be of tremendous benefits to you now and forever.

When one talks of LOVE, people have different definitions of it. Some people describe 'love' as a strong **feeling** that binds people together. Others define it as a mixture of acceptable beliefs, behaviors, and emotion.

Also, some people say there are three types of love, and they list them as follows: romantic love, family/brotherly love, and God's divine love.

Obviously, LOVE has been greatly misunderstood, misused, misinterpreted, and mistaken to the point it lost its essence. And because of these varying definitions, there is a prevailing confusion and misunderstanding of LOVE. These misconceptions have crippled and ruined untold number of relationships, even more so today.

But, just as the title of this Book says, 'The Blooming Love', you are going to see today what LOVE really is, and how it works in a relationship to bring enormous happiness, attraction, enthusiasm, liveliness and peace to your relationship.

But before we go into that, let's quickly see what LOVE is not, so to clear those misconceptions about it. Here are some:

1. Love is not an emotion in itself nor is it a desire, lust, and infatuation. You can like someone's physical attributes like eye color, height, body shape, nose shape, dimples, etc. You can like their educational status, high occupation and income, social status, the special skill they possess, etc., but that is not love of the person or for the person.
   In romantic arena, liking the things of a person means you want what he/she possesses. That's it!
   Now, there is nothing wrong with liking what someone possesses, but to call it LOVE is wrong. And why is it wrong? It is because such feeling of yours is self-centered and not LOVE for the other person.
2. Love is not a shared or mutual sexual emotion.
3. **Sex** is not love, and love is not sex. Romance is not love. The fact that someone

4

sleeps with you or you sleep with someone is not an indication of the presence of love. Intense physical attraction towards someone is not love.

4. Love is not using endearment words like honey, dear, babe, etc. to address your spouse.
5. Physical touch by itself is not love for the other person; but LOVE for the other person can result to physical touch.

So then, what is love?

CHAPTER 1

What is LOVE?

'LOVE' is **actions** rather than words. Why? It is because one can have good intentions (mental) towards someone, but if that good intention does not guide your behavior towards the person, then the good intention is zero.

And there are characteristics you must display to show you actually love someone. These traits are described in the scriptures as follows:

"Love is patient, <u>love is kind</u>. It does not envy, it does not boast, it is not proud. It is not rude, it is not self-seeking, it is not easily angered, it keeps no account of wrongs. Love takes no pleasure in evil,

but rejoices in the truth."
– 1 Corinthians 13:4-6

And what does it mean to be 'KIND?' To be considered 'kind', a person must exhibit the following actions:

- ✓ **Caring** for the other person
- ✓ **Being sensitive** towards the other person
- ✓ **Considerate** of the other person
- ✓ **Helpful** to the other person
- ✓ **Thoughtful** of the other person
- ✓ **Selfless** – sacrificing your time and energy for the other person
- ✓ **Cooperative** with the other person
- ✓ **Attentive** to the other person
- ✓ **Compassionate** towards the other person
- ✓ **Sympathetic** towards the other person
- ✓ **Having understanding** towards the other person
- ✓ **Friendly** with the other person
- ✓ **Courteous** to the other person
- ✓ **Agreeable** with the other person
- ✓ **Pleasant** towards the other person

- ✓ **Generous** towards the other person
- ✓ **Merciful, pitying** towards the other person
- ✓ **Giving** to the other person.

In other words, here is what 'LOVE' is:

> # LOVE is a powerful sense of empathy toward another person where you are willing and **moved** to sacrifice your time and efforts for the person.

- ✓ Isn't that what JESUS did by accepting to come to earth to die for the sins of man?

And here is what GOD said:

"Be kind one to another…"
- Ephesians 4:32

✳✳✳

Reader, but here comes the problem in relationships, and that is, a lot of people just want to be on the receiving end, and they do not realize that LOVE is a two-way street, and also that it has two parts to it.

Absolutely, 'LOVE' is made up of two parts, and they are:

   1) **Unconditional** love, and
   2) **Conditional** love

These two parts must be at play in a relationship for LOVE to be complete. If only one part is practiced in a relationship, that relationship is bound to fall apart and doomed. So, if a union is going to survive, thrive, and happy both parts must be applied.

Please note: Here, we are talking about regular, continuous, adult-to-adult relationships, and not with random people you come across or young children.

Someone once said that "Real love is unconditional, and that this is the type of love everybody wants." In other words, he was saying that everybody wants free things. Of course, everybody wants free things, but that is not how GOD, the CREATOR, set up LOVE to work between and among people. Similarly, that is not how GOD set up LOVE to work between Himself and humans. But prosperity Preachers have been deceiving people by telling them GOD loves you unconditionally if you can just concentrate on having lots of faith to get things from GOD.

The word, 'Unconditional', means you do not have to work for the love you want from the other person; but you want the other person to work to give you free love. Isn't that an inconsiderate mindset?

Now, in order to understand LOVE, let us see how GOD, Himself, practices love because He said humans should imitate Him. Here is the verse:

"Therefore be imitators of God as dear children." - Ephesians 5:1

CHAPTER 2

How GOD Practices LOVE

GOD is LOVE, and He is the author of LOVE.
GOD has two parts to the love He exercises
towards every human, and they are:

1. **Unconditional** part, and
2. **Conditional** part

And, as you saw earlier, those two parts must be
together for love to be complete. The following is
an example of His **unconditional** love:

- PROVISIONS – GOD provides resources. He
  created the earth and put everything needed
  to survive on it for everybody, regardless of
  who is moral or immoral. GOD knows,
  without these supplies, humans would not
  survive. So, He provides these things without
  requiring humans to meet any standard of
  His, with the exception of when He is

executing judgments. Here is an example of that love:

"... He causes His sun to rise on the evil and the good, and sends rain on the righteous and the unrighteous."
- Matthew 5:44-45

And just as that verse says, it does not matter if people love Him or not; He still needs to do what He has to do for the earth.

And besides providing resources, He also does random acts of kindness to people who do not love Him. But sadly, this type of unconditional love is the only love most people want from GOD. And equally saddening, it is the same unconditional love they only want from other people in relationships, whether the relationship is between husband and wife, parents and older children, platonic friends, etc. Now, why is that? It is because 'unconditional love' does not cost them any efforts, time, or money.

But it is foolhardy, thoughtless, and self-centered to want someone to only love you unconditionally.

And it is also foolhardy, thoughtless, and self-centered to want GOD to only love you unconditionally.

Now, having seen the unconditional love of GOD, let us then see His **conditional love.** Here it is in the following verses:

"Now therefore, if you will obey my voice indeed, and keep my covenant, then you shall be a peculiar treasure unto me above all people: for all the earth is mine." - Exodus 19:5

"So he went out to meet Asa and said to him, "Listen to me, Asa and all Judah and Benjamin. The LORD is with you when you are with Him. If you seek Him,

He will be found by you, but if you forsake Him, He will forsake you. "
- 2 Chronicles 15:2

"See, today I am setting before you a blessing and a curse - a blessing if you obey the commandments of the LORD your God that I am giving you today, but a curse if you disobey the commandments of the LORD your God and turn aside from the path I command you today by following other gods, which you have not known."

- Deuteronomy 11:26-28

Reader, we hope you caught the word 'if' in those verses above. 'If' is conditional, right? It is very clear in those verses that GOD set up a condition or requirement to be met before receiving His other benefits or blessings.

Also, **it is GOD'S <u>conditional love</u> that separates people going to heaven from the people going to hell.**

In fact, all GOD'S blessings are conditional aside from His provision of general resources for all humans and His random acts of kindness. But prosperity Preachers will not tell you that. They just paint a free-for-all picture about GOD to excite and arouse you in their churches and in social media so you can give more tithes and offerings, and become their follower for more money. But those types of preaching have led to churches producing mostly ungodly, Christians-in-name-only people.

And here is the thing –When you want to be in a Father/son relationship with GOD and JESUS, you have to wholeheartedly desire to obey whatever He tells you in order for the relationship with Him to survive. In other words, you have to work for His love just as He works to gain your love. Here are some of the verses:

"We love Him because He first loved us." - 1 John 4:19

"Or do you show contempt for the riches of his kindness, forbearance and patience, not realizing that God's kindness is intended to lead you to repentance?" - Romans 2:4

➢ GOD works to get your love.

Indeed, it is GOD'S goodness to everyone that brings him/her to repentance. The question is, has GOD ever done anything for you in life? Here is a quick reminder of one of the things He does for you, and that is, He woke you up this morning. But, lots of people just take things for granted. That is why they do not appreciate GOD for what He is doing for them every day.

Surely, GOD practices what He has preached. But there are people who deceive themselves thinking GOD'S unconditional love, called grace (unmerited favor) will gain them entrance to heaven or bring GOD'S blessings to them. That is a self-destroying, self-limiting belief and assumption. Why? It is because you are not working to earn your love from GOD and JESUS. Here is what Apostle Paul said regarding that:

"As the body without the spirit is dead, so faith without works is dead."
- James 2:26

The same goes for human relationships, and that is, if you are not making efforts to earn love from the other person, then that relationship is doomed for failure.

Reader, do you know that your works (obedience of GOD'S laws) are being recorded daily in your book? Certainly, GOD is keeping track of your daily actions, whether good or evil. Therefore, on the judgment day, JESUS is going to judge you out of what is written in your Book. Here are the verses:

"Then I saw a great white throne and the One seated on it. Earth and heaven (the universe) *fled from His presence, and no place was found for them. And I saw the dead, great and small, standing before the throne. And there were open books, and one of them was the Book of Life. And the dead were judged according to their deeds, as recorded in the books. The sea gave up its dead, and Death and Hades gave up their dead, and each one was judged according to his deeds. Then Death and Hades were thrown into the lake of fire. This is the second death—the*

lake of fire."
- Revelation 20:11-14

So, when you call yourself a 'Christian' you must sincerely commit to obeying GOD/JESUS' commandments because **that is the only way you show to GOD and JESUS you love them.** Here is the verse:

"If you love Me, you will keep My commandments." - John 14:15

And here are examples of those commandments:

"For out of the heart come evil thoughts, murder, adultery, sexual immorality, theft, false testimony, and slander."
- Matthew 15:19

"The acts of the flesh are obvious: sexual immorality, impurity, and corruption; idolatry and sorcery; hatred,

discord, jealousy, and rage; rivalries, divisions, factions." - Galatians 5:19

And here are the fruits a commandment-obeying Christian must have:

"But the fruit of the Spirit is love, joy, peace, patience, kindness, goodness, faithfulness, gentleness, and self-control. Against such things there is no law. Those who belong to Christ Jesus have crucified the flesh with its passions and desires." - Galatians 5:23

GOD is the PARENT, and He wants to be obeyed. In the physical realm, apart from GOD instructing children to obey their earthly parents, cultures around the world teach children to obey their parents also. Why will anyone then think GOD should not be obeyed? And why will anyone think he/she will escape not being punished by GOD for not obeying Him?

***

Indeed, it is when you LOVE GOD by following his rules that He will eagerly love you back. And in the same way, when you go out of your way to do things and be kind to your partner, that is when the love between both of you blossoms, succeeds, happy and peaceful.

Certainly, you will not get special love from GOD when you are only under his unconditional love. It will not happen. Here are the verses:

"I love those who love me, and those who seek me find me." Proverbs 8:17

"The LORD tests the righteous, But the wicked and the one who loves violence His soul hates." - Psalm 11:5

Reader, from that last verse, you can see that GOD does not love everybody besides giving them general necessities like the rain and the sun.

***

And here is what goes with obeying GOD'S commandments, and that is, the TRUST of GOD. GOD wants you to trust Him. Another word for TRUST is FAITH. TRUST is so important to GOD that the LACK OF IT IS SIN. Here is the verse:

"… and everything that does not come from faith is sin." - Romans 14:23

For example, part of the reasons GOD prevented the children of Israel (the adults, with the exception of Joshua and Caleb) from entering the Promised Land was lack of trust of Him.

And for a true Christian, the Promised Land is heaven, starting from here. Therefore, not trusting GOD or not living by faith will prevent you from entering heaven. GOD IS NO RESPECTER OF

PERSONS. If He did it to the children of Israel, He will do it to you.

Actually, trusting GOD is a command from GOD, and not a suggestion. Here is what He said:

"...The just shall live by faith."
- Romans 1:17

Also, this is why the scripture says "without faith, it is impossible to please GOD. Here is the verse:

"And without faith it is impossible to please God, because anyone who comes to him must believe that he exists and that he rewards those who earnestly seek him." - Hebrews 11:6

And here are some other verses about trusting GOD:

"Offer the sacrifices of righteousness, and put your trust in the LORD."
- Psalm 4:5

"Trust in the LORD, and do good; so shalt thou dwell in the land, and verily thou shalt be fed." - Psalm 37:3

"Trust in the LORD with all your heart; and lean not on your own understanding." - Proverbs 3:5

Please note: **Faith alone will not get you to heaven.** Here is the verse:

"So too, faith by itself, if it does not result in action, is dead." - James 2:17

LOVE IS

↓

1. **Conditional**
   - Merited
   - Give and Receive

----

2. **Unconditional**
   - Unmerited

Now, let's quickly see some of the characteristics of the people who crave unconditional love from GOD and from people:

CHAPTER 3

Characteristics of the Desirers of Unconditional Love

---

1. They have the spirit of entitlement.

They feel, just by being in close relationship with you, you are supposed to do the following for them, regardless of how badly they treat you, and how unconcerned they are towards you. They expect you to:

- Automatically forgive them without them repenting and asking for forgiveness - they want you to sweep all their wrongdoings to you under the carpet. That is why they are very defensive when you point out their faults. And instead of them to be apologetic, they will turn the table on you by being angry for not forgiving them sooner. They will forcefully try to make you the offender and they the victims.

- Have guaranteed friendliness towards them.
- Be good to them always.
- Be available anytime to serve them.
- Be kind to them.
- Be respectful or honor them.
- Be of benefits to them in any way possible.
- Be of guaranteed support emotionally, monetarily or otherwise to them.
- Satisfy them in any area.
- Accommodate them anytime.
  Etc.

2. They are always not grateful or not genuinely grateful. This is the offshoot of entitlement spirit. Some of them blatantly will not acknowledge what you have done for them.

And for some of them, even when they say "thank you," they are saying it because culture says you should say "thank you. But deep down in their hearts, they are not actually grateful because they feel you are supposed to do the favor for them anyway.

3. They have no inner inhibitions in asking you to do things for them because they do not care about how their requests will affect you.

But a child of GOD will not do that. Now, before a person of GOD asks another person to do things for him/her, he/she will consider how such request will affect that person. But for users (the enthusiasts of unconditional love), they have no problem asking you for favors, and they will ask you with bold face.

4. They are never satisfied, no matter how much you do for them,

even when you are going through pains to help them. They will never see your pains and sacrifice.

Reader, do you know where they got that insatiable mindset from? It is from their leader and father, the devil. See below what GOD did in heaven for the then-angel Lucifer, now the devil, Here is GOD speaking to the devil:

"You were in Eden, the garden of God. Every kind of precious stone adorned you: ruby, topaz, and diamond, beryl, onyx, and jasper, sapphire, turquoise, and emerald. Your mountings and settings were crafted in gold, prepared on the day of your creation. You were anointed as a guardian cherub, for I had ordained you. You were on the holy mountain of God; you walked among the fiery stones. From the day you were created you were blameless in your ways—until wickedness was found in you." - Ezekiel 28:13-15

Therefore, do not be surprised when you are doing things for your spouse or someone else and he/she is never satisfied, no matter your efforts to please him/her. It is not a new mindset.

✳✳✳

Here is another thing about unconditional love: below are some of what you are going to live with the rest of your life if you base your relationship with GOD and JESUS **only** on unconditional love from Him:

- **Daily unhappiness**
- **Feeling of emptiness**
- **Lack of inner peace**
- **Life uncertainty**
- **Fragmented inner being instead of being whole**
- **Physically and emotionally beaten-up**
- **Inner loneliness**
- **Depression**, etc., and then,
- **Condemnation to hell fire by GOD at the end.**

But here are some of your benefits when you are living with GOD/JESUS under **His conditional** love, which is the opposite of His unconditional love:

- ✓ **Daily happiness**
- ✓ **Peace within your being**

- ✓ **Wholesome, well-rounded, solid, complete life**
- ✓ **Assurance of life**
- ✓ **No feeling of loneliness**
- ✓ **Spiritually and emotionally sound,** etc., and at the end, you will have a
- ✓ **Celebrated welcome by GOD to His residence, heaven.**

$$ * * * $$

So, thus far, we have looked at LOVE and how GOD, Himself, practices love. We also touched briefly above on how LOVE works among humans. Now, we are going to see in depth, how love works among humans:

CHAPTER 4

How Love Works Among Humans

As you read above, the way LOVE works with GOD, that is how it works with man. And just as many people want only unconditional love from GOD, that is what they desire from fellow humans also.

Besides, one of the most powerful words that attracts people is 'Free." People want to get things free instead of working for them. That is why you usually hear them say "marriage is hard." Why do they say marriage is hard? It is because they do not want to work for the love they want from their spouses. In order words, they want to be loved UNCONDITIONALLY just as they want GOD to love them unconditionally. These people are self-centered, to say the least. Here are examples of how self-centeredness is displayed in different relationships:

Spouses: A self-centered spouse is inconsiderate, unfeeling, thoughtless, and hard-hearted in relating to you during the day, but when night comes, he/she wants you to sleep with him/her because he/she has the right to your body under marriage certificate.

But what these self-centered spouses do not realize is that operating from entitlement mindset will result to the following in a marriage:

- Resentments
- Constant quarreling and fighting
- Emotional disconnect
- Lack of intimacy
- Lack of trust
- Loneliness
- Anger
  Etc.

Siblings: Your siblings want you to do things for them because you are from the same parents, regardless of how unwilling they are to help you when you need help.

And here are some of the results from relating to your siblings expecting only unconditional love from them:

- Resentments
- Anger
- Lack of trust
- Emotional disconnect
- Physical distance
  Etc.

In-laws: You have in-laws who want you to always do things for them or give to them without them doing the same to you.

Now, here are some of the results from relating to your in-laws expecting only unconditional love:

- Physical distance
- Lack of trust
- Anger
- Resentment
  Etc.

Platonic friends: You have a friend who wants you to always call her to see how she is doing, but he/she will never remember to call you sometimes. Here are some of the results from relating to a friend expecting only unconditional love:

- Lack of trust
- Physical distance, etc.

Absolutely, GOD did not create LOVE to work on uneven or imbalanced basis. Please note: we are not talking of an ounce for an ounce here, or "I gave you $10, therefore you have to give me $10 back." No. We are talking about you making efforts to also do things for the other person from love.

Also, in terms of doing things for people and treating them right, it is crucial you do all things from LOVE for people, and not to buy future help from them. That is what unbelievers do, which is, they help and give to you so they can get from you in future. <u>A moral person gives and helps because they are the right things to do.</u>

The point is, are you willing to sacrifice for the other person as he/she is willing to sacrifice for you?

Therefore, in acting from love in relationships, do the following:

- ✓ When someone shows empathy towards you, you need to show empathy to him/her.
- ✓ When someone is considerate of you, you need to be considerate towards him/her.

- ✓ When someone gives to you (time, efforts, substances, etc.), you need to give to the person in any way also.
- ✓ When someone takes time to listen to your problems and renders help, you need to do the same to the person when he/she needs listening ears.
- ✓ When someone willingly helps you, you need to willingly help him/her also.
- ✓ When someone is respectful of you, you need to respect him/her too.
- ✓ When someone is willing to bear your burden, you should be willing to bear his/her burden when needed also.
- ✓ When someone remembers to celebrate your birthday, for instance, you need to remember to celebrate his/her birthday without being reminded to do so also.
  Etc.

Here is an example of love in action - **giving.** Love gives. When you are in a relationship, you need to give to the other person. And when you are in relationship with GOD, you need to give back to GOD as He gives to you. Here is one of His giving:

"For GOD so loved the world that He gave His only Begotten Son."
- John 3:16

That simply means you cannot just be at the receiving end and not be willing to give to the other person.

And here is the fact about GIVING, and that is, LOVE does not give with the intention to receive back. Again, <u>LOVE gives because it is the right thing to do. The other person also should do the same because it is the right thing to do.</u>

If you give with the intention to receive back, then, that is a self-centered giving, and not acting from love. GOD gives and shows kindness not because He wants to get back. He does so because it is the right thing to do; and that is LOVE.

A relationship is a two-way street of GIVING and RECEIVING - all coming from LOVE. That is how GOD created relationship to be.

Now, with regards to giving back to GOD, we are not talking about giving tithes and offerings, helping people, or doing other charitable works in the name of GOD and JESUS. While it is highly praiseworthy to help the poor and the needy, the fact is, when you do those good things, you are laying up treasures in heaven. In other words, in heaven, GOD will repay you with treasures for doing them for people. So, when you do those things, you are doing them for yourself also, though you are acting from empathy for the people.

So then, what is GIVING TO GOD?

Giving to GOD is when you do something that directly goes to Him. What then do you do that directly benefits GOD? It is WORSHIP /PRAISE.

"Why worship and praise?" you may ask. The reason is, it took GOD six days to put on earth everything one would need to survive on it. For example, can you live without air to breathe in?

QUESTION – Does GOD deserve a "thank you" or something? Certainly! But GOD is self-sufficient. He does not eat food, so you cannot give Him food. He does not need money, so you cannot give Him money. But He must enjoy something, right? Absolutely! He desires PRAISES of Him.

But when one talks of PRAISE, it is not singing motivational songs in the church: for example, when a church is singing a song that says 'We shall meet again one day.' That is not praising GOD. That is a song to uplift fellow Christians.

Also, besides you personally praising Him in your daily living, it is time for churches to separate songs that motivate one another from songs dedicated to praise GOD. There is time to motivate one another, and there is time to PRAISE GOD. Here is an example of a PRAISE song - the title is "How Great Thou Art." Here is the beginning of the song:

How Great Thou Art
Oh Lord my God,
When I in awesome wonder
Etc.

Carl Boberg (1885)

When you look at the entire lyrics of that song, you will find that the author praised GOD from the beginning to the end.

Below is another example of a PRAISE song.

Great is Thy faithfulness

Great is Thy faithfulness, O God my Father
There is no shadow of turning with Thee
Thou changest not, Thy compassions, they fail not
As Thou hast been, Thou forever will be

Great is Thy faithfulness
Great is Thy faithfulness
Morning by morning new mercies I see
All I have needed Thy hand hath provided
Great is Thy faithfulness, Lord, unto me
Etc.

(Written by Thomas Chisholm, Published by Hope Publishing, 1923)

All right, that is GIVING BACK TO GOD because a relationship is GIVE and TAKE, all coming from LOVE for the other person.

So, are both types of songs needed in the church? Absolutely! True Christians need to praise GOD and they also need to motivate one another. But churches need to call spade a spade. Lots of churches sing motivational songs and call them 'praise and worship.' The word 'worship' means praise and honor and not inspiring one another.

JESUS is the example for Christians, right? How about we look at the way JESUS related to GOD when He was on earth. See below how He praised GOD in the LORD'S PRAYER which He taught Christians:

"<u>After this manner therefore pray ye</u>:
Our Father which art in heaven,
Hallowed be thy name.
Thy kingdom come, Thy will be done on earth, as it is in heaven.
Give us this day our daily bread.
And forgive us our trespasses as we forgive them that trespass against us.

And lead us not into temptation, but deliver us from evil: For thine is the kingdom, and the power, and the glory, forever. Amen."   *- Matthew 6:9-13*

Reader, when you look at that prayer, you see that it is a GIVE and RECEIVE meeting. It started with PRAISES TO GOD by saying *"Our Father which art in heaven, Hallowed be thy name."*

To hallow someone is to praise, respect, revere, and extol the person's magnificent virtues. There in the prayer, JESUS gave to GOD first before asking from GOD. Doesn't that show that GOD ALSO DESIRES SOMETHING? Indeed, He desires PRAISES.

Moreover, notice also how JESUS ended the prayer. What did He do? He gladdened GOD'S heart by acknowledging His broad possession, the KINGDOM; and then praised His power and His magnificence. It was only in-between those two praises in the prayer that JESUS requested GOD to do something.

So, why did JESUS do that? It is because there is a relationship between GOD and His children. When you are in a relationship with GOD as a Christian, you have to give to GOD as He gives to you from LOVE; if not, that relationship will not survive. When former angel Lucifer was in heaven, after a while, he refused to give back to GOD, among his other sins, and he was cast out of heaven.

A true Christian needs to praise GOD for one reason or the other in his/her daily living.
And do you know that GOD actually cherishes the praises from you? See what He does when you praise Him:

"But thou art holy, You who inhabits the praises of Your people." - Psalm 22:3

So, when you praise GOD, He comes to where the praises are being offered. Isn't that amazing to find something you can give back to GOD when He has been giving to you generously?

***

And with regards to **giving** among people, here is the thing, and that is, know when to give and when not to give. Know when to help and when not to help, etc. Wisdom from GOD will help you know when and when not.

Do compare the following two verses from JESUS with regards to giving:

"Give to those who ask, and don't turn away from those who want to borrow."
- Matthew 5:42

"Do not give what is holy to the dogs; nor cast your pearls before swine, lest they trample them under their feet, and turn and tear you in pieces."
- Matthew 7:6

Is it not the same JESUS talking? Certainly! Discernment will help you know when to apply which.

Again, please note that we are not talking here about helping, giving and caring for random people or when you are led by GOD to help, give, or care for someone. We are talking about continuing relationships.

Therefore, in any ongoing relationship, do not aid and abet perpetual bad behaviors from people. Know when to be close to people and know when to keep them far from you. Know when to help them and when not to help them.

Know when to apply unconditional love and when they should earn their love from you (conditional).

Inconsiderate people always ask GOD to give and give to them, but they will never consider how they can give to GOD.

Moreover, the people who only want unconditional love in human relationships do the same to GOD. When you are in a relationship with them, it is all about what they can get from you, and not how they too can be of benefits to you.

Now, in giving and helping other people, while it is true you are to give and lend freely, but be aware of users because if you give to them once, they will keep on asking from you over and over again without any consideration. This is why GOD wants you to know the following about them; here it is:

"The <u>leech has two daughters - Give and Give!</u> There are three things that are never satisfied. Four never say, "Enough!" - Proverbs 30:15

Therefore, beware of leeches or moochers when it comes to lending and giving.

Certainly, it is time to stop using GOD by not obeying Him, and it is time to stop using people.

JESUS said:

"Do to others whatever you would like them do to you. This is the essence of all that is taught in the law and the prophets." - Matthew 7:12

Here again are the two components of LOVE:

Unconditional Love

+

Conditional Love

=

***Complete* LOVE**

Here are examples of when **unconditional** love is applied in human relationships:

✓ If you see the other person is in harm's way, it is mandatory for you to pull him/her out of it, with no condition attached.

✓ If a person is hungry or thirsty and cannot meet his/her needs, and you are in the position to supply those needs, it is mandatory you do so without condition attached.

✓ Forgiveness - Forgiving the other person can be unconditional or conditional, but JESUS would rather want you to forgive unconditionally. Here is what JESUS said about forgiving the other person, and that is, a condition has to be met by the person:

"Even if they sin against you seven times in a day and seven times come back to you saying 'I repent,' you must forgive them."
- Luke 17:4

"Take heed to yourselves: If your brother sins against you, rebuke

him; <u>and if he repents</u>, forgive him."
- Luke 17:3

So, as you saw above, JESUS said when the offender comes back to you and says he/she repents, then you must forgive.
But Christians-in-name-only usually quote the part of the verse that says "forgive." And you always hear them preach 'forgive, forgive, forgive,' but they will never quote the part that says **"I repent," "I repent."** Why? It is because they, themselves, do not want to repent. They put the burden on the victim to change, and not the offender to repent and stop offending people purposely.

But on the other hand, forgiveness is unconditional. Here are the verses:

"But if you do not forgive others their sins, your Father will not forgive your sins." - Matthew 6:15

"And forgive us our sins, as we also have forgiven those who sin against us. - Matthew 6:12

You need to forgive even when the other person refuses to repent. Please understand that forgiving the other person is not solely for them; it is also for you. Why? It is because you do not want to harbor dirt in your body. Unforgiveness is dirt. Nevertheless, Preachers need to teach their followers to stop offending others purposely.

Also, from your experience, you know that most of your offenders do not ask for forgiveness, ever, right? Therefore, whether the offender says "I am sorry" or not, you have to forgive because JESUS said they do not know what they are doing. (Luke 23:34).

And how do you forgive the other person? You pray for him/her by asking GOD to open that person's spiritual eyes because he/she is definitely blind for deliberately offending you.

Absolutely, it hurts when someone intentionally offends you. That is why JESUS pronounced "woe" on the offender. Here is the verse:

"Woe to the world because of offenses! For offenses must come, but woe to that man by whom the offense comes!" - Matthew 18:7

So, what is 'woe?' It is – sorrow, misery, distress, unhappiness, heartache, despair, dejection, depression, gloom, melancholy, misfortune, disaster, affliction, suffering, hardship, pain, grief, torment, etc. Who then wants 'woe' in his/her life? Nobody! So, if you do not want 'woe' in your life, then stay away from purposely offending other people in any shape or form. GOD has pronounced the consequences, and they must happen to the offender – guaranteed.

Now, here is the confusion lots of people have when it comes to forgiveness, and that is, they mistakenly think when you forgive someone, it automatically means both of you become close again. No! It is not always so. You can forgive someone in your heart, but then keep them far from you to avoid future offenses, especially when they cannot see the errors of their ways.

But there are people who offend you, and afterwards become sincerely regretful of it. Those are the people you can become close to again. Nevertheless, you need to be discerning because there are people who would say "sorry" to you, but they do not actually mean it. To them, it is a game and a strategy to be close to you again because they want to gain from you. Watch out for those types of cunning offenders because they are bound to continue to offend you over and over again without sincerely repenting.

Definitely, JESUS wants you to forgive, but He also wants you to use wisdom to know who to be closed to and who to be far from. In fact, anyone who continuously offends you purposely is an unbeliever; and this is why GOD said you should distance yourself from that unbeliever. Here is the verse:

"Do not be yoked together with unbelievers. For what do righteousness and wickedness have

in common? Or what fellowship can light have with darkness?"
- 2 Corinthians 6:14

Here, you may ask "What about my spouse who is always offending me? What do I do?" Now, with regards to spouses, first of all, you should not have married someone who is not a commandment-obeying person as the verse above says. But you did not know that then, and now that you are married to him/her, and you are personally obeying GOD'S commandments, GOD will tell you what to do or how to manage the relationship.

***

Alright, now that we are talking about marriage, let's quickly look at how conditional and unconditional love affect love-making in marriage:

CHAPTER 5

How Conditional and Unconditional Love Affect Love-making in a Marriage

This is an area that causes huge problems in marriages due to the application of conditional and unconditional love in the relationship. In marriages, lots of people use their marriage license as an entitlement to compulsory lovemaking with the other partner. In other words, these people feel they are entitled to the sexual activities in their marriages regardless of how inconsiderate, uncaring, unhelpful, and irresponsible they are in relating to the other person. And that is wrong! The people who demand sexual involvements from their spouses, when they are self-centered, have entitlement attitudes. Here are more of what they do also in marriages:

- The men are not willing to provide for their wives and children, and the women are not willing to cook, clean, and take care of the children.
- The men are not willing to help out in the home when help is needed, and the women are not willing to help the men when they need help.
- They are not willing to help raise the children.
- They always nag the other spouse unjustifiably because they are never satisfied no matter the efforts you put in.
- They are inconsiderate - everything has to go their way.
- The marriage is only about them and the families they come from, and nothing else matters to them.
- They are not willing to give, but want to receive.
- They are not willing to honor and respect you, whether behind closed doors or outside, especially in the presence of their relatives and friends; but they want you to honor and respect them.

Etc.

So, with regards to love-making, you are now going to see what Apostle Paul said in the scriptures. Why is this important to know? It is because a lot of people who call themselves Christians have misused the scripture below to take advantage of their spouses. They approach their partners with the attitude of "your body belongs to me," therefore, you have to give in on demand."

Here is what Apostle Paul said:

"But because there is so much sexual immorality, each man should have his own wife, and each woman her own husband. <u>The husband should fulfill his marital duty to his wife, and likewise the wife to her husband</u>. The wife does not have authority over her own body, but the husband. Likewise, the husband does not have authority over his own body, but the wife. Do not deprive each other, except by mutual consent and for a time, so you may devote yourselves to prayer. Then come together again, so that Satan

will not tempt you through your lack of self-control. I say this as a concession, not as a command."
- 1 Corinthians 7:2-6

You see, GOD does not contradict Himself and He is the GOD of JUSTICE. Looking at that passage, you saw how Apostle Paul first reinforced the fact that the husband should fulfill his marital duty to his wife, and likewise the wife to her husband, right? Absolutely, when you sign on to a marriage relationship, you are accepting the responsibilities that go with it. And GOD, who knows it all, has already divided the responsibilities between the man and the woman in the scriptures. By the way, if you want to know how GOD divided the responsibilities, read our other book titled (**Relationship Should Be 50/50 If Not It Won't Work**). In that Book, among other things, you will see the responsibilities assigned to each partner in the marriage.

So, as a spouse, you must make sure you are fulfilling your responsibilities to your partner if you are going to expect lovemaking from him/her.

Secondly, Apostle Paul concluded by saying that lovemaking in marriage comes out of agreement, and not out of compulsion, nor is it a law. Here is what he said again: *"I say this as a concession, not as a command."*

But what happens in a lot of marriages is the expectation of **unconditional love** from the other spouse when they, themselves, do not want to get out of their ways to do the right things or say the right things to their spouses.

People do not want to be inconvenienced to do things so love can flourish. These people mentally live in fantasy island by expecting their marriages to magically be enjoyable, agreeable, pleasurable, humorous and happy without them putting in efforts to make that happen.

Therefore, if you, as a spouse, has been inconsiderate, unhelpful, self-centered, unsympathetic, uncaring, and insensitive towards your spouse during the day, why are you surprised or angry when you get rejected by your spouse at night?

But even so, some spouses, especially women who are badly treated by their spouses may still surrender their bodies to their husbands to prevent them from stepping outside the marriage. But what will happen then is that these women are not emotional involved in the lovemaking process. They are just submitting their bodies without excitement because the other spouse is inconsiderate, self-centered, and hard-hearted.

Therefore, here is your obligation if you want your spouse to be involved bodily and emotionally in lovemaking with you, and that is:

  ✓ Do the right things to your spouse.

✳✳✳

In general, applying only unconditional love is for babies and random acts of kindness or for other special cases when someone is incapacitated. But, even for the children, as they grow older, parents start to apply conditional love. They have been doing so from the beginning of time. For example, you can refuse to buy a new toy for a child if he/she refuses to keep his/her room tidy, etc.

But with regards to parenting, what is appalling is when some parents exercise their conditional love in terrible ways towards their teenagers and call it 'tough love.' Here are some examples:

➤ Because your teenager does not obey you, you throw him/her out of your house. Now, that is wrong!
When you do that, where do you expect this child of yours to live or sleep? The street? The other option is, these teenagers could end up in the hands of human predators that will use them as sex slaves. Throwing your teenagers out of the house is a wrong application of conditional love.

➤ Also, there are some parents who would stop giving their teenagers money for their necessities in order to break them. But you know that these teenagers are not working yet, and that you are their only source for money. But then, you capitalize on that edge you have over them, to punish and chase them to the streets. That is immoral!

Here is a true story – one Sunday, a parent was preparing to go to a church service, but he had a problem with his teenager. So, what did he do? He locked the door to prevent the teenager from coming in to the house and he went to church.

Now, that was a wrong application of conditional love or tough love. If it is you, would you want that done to you? Those types of acts are evil at the highest level. What happens to *"Do to others what you want done to you"*?

As a parent, there are many rightful ways to apply conditional love to your teenagers, but they do not include denial of food, money for necessities, and chasing them out of the house.

But Reader, here is the fact about human nature, and that is, without you being led by GOD and JESUS, you cannot rightfully determine when and how to apply conditional or unconditional love in a relationship. Anything short of GOD and JESUS, you are bound to continue to **mismanage** your relationships – guaranteed.

And that is why we need to end this topic of LOVE with GOD again since He is the designer of love, so you can start to imitate Him. Therefore, you are now going to see what GOD wants from you when you are in a relationship with Him. Here it is:

When GOD loves you, you must love Him back.

Certainly, **GOD wants to be loved too.** That is why it is the first and the greatest commandment. Here it is:

"Jesus declared, "'Love the Lord your God with all your heart and with all your soul and with all your mind.' This is the first and greatest commandment. And the second is like it: 'Love your neighbor as yourself.' All the Law and the Prophets hang on these two commandments."
- Matthew 22:38-39

GOD knows what He wants. But a lot of people want to love GOD the way they want. Isn't that amazing? See again below how GOD wants you to love Him:

"If you love Me, keep My commandments." - John 14:15

GOD is specific in that verse. The **only way** you show GOD and JESUS you love them is by

OBEYING HIS COMMANDMENTS. You cannot love them in any other way.

But some people are ungrateful, self-centered, careless, dissatisfied and demanding that they forget that the breath they have today is a gift from GOD. They forget they are using everything that belongs to GOD here on earth – the water, sun, mineral resources and everything on earth. How can you be using someone's things and you go against Him by breaking His laws?

GOD is the LANDLORD of planet earth. This is why He made the rules (laws or commandments) for the people to live by so there will be peace and happiness on earth! Is that not what human landlords also do? Why is it that some people blatantly want to make their own rules and do the opposite of what GOD said? The worse thing is that some people are proud disobeying GOD. But what they do not know is, the moment they draw their last breath on earth, the devil will come to get their spirits to a hot hell where there is no single drop of water to quench their thirst as a consequence for challenging GOD and His laws.

Surely, the moment you draw your last breath on earth, there will be no lawyer or group of supporters to save you from GOD'S punishment. When you disobey GOD, you are done!!

But here is how the devil deceives people – He convinces them to "enjoy" life to the fullest here on earth right now, with complete disregard for GOD'S laws, then die, and that will be the end of it all for them. **But that is not the end of it all for them!** <u>These people do not know that they are being deceived by the devil.</u> Reader, here is the fact, and that is, there is no enjoyment for purposely-sinning people. These people do not have peace daily here on earth. GOD set it up that way, and no one or anything can change it. Here is the verse:

"There is no peace," says the LORD, "for the wicked." - Isaiah 48:22

And here is a quick definition of 'wickedness.' 'Wickedness' is when you know what is right, but you purposely do the opposite.

So, where is the enjoyment coming from when you do not have peace and happiness in life? Is it the fly-away, temporary drop of happiness a person gets from sexual immorality, stepping on others to get ahead, making lots of money through corrupt ways and then travel the whole world, have fleet of cars, jet planes, etc.? You can travel to the moon, or be at all the beautiful beaches in the world, for example, still, there will be no peace and happiness for you if you are purposely breaking GOD'S laws. The only people who enjoy beaches, for example, are those with clean hearts.

✳✳✳

Also, Reader, do you know that spirits do not die? Absolutely, your spirit will not die. What enables you to move around is your spirit within you, **and that spirit is the real you.** That spirit will never die. That is why when someone passes away, people say he/she has departed. Who departed when the body is still lying there? It is the spirit of the person that departed.

Now, it is that spirit that gets judged immediately after you draw your last breath on earth. How do we know that? See below what JESUS told the **former** thief that was on the cross beside Him, before they all died on their crosses:

"Jesus answered him, "Truly I tell you, <u>today</u> you will be with me in paradise."
- Luke 23:43

That immediate judgment is to separate the good spirits from the bad ones, and to send each spirit to the appropriate, temporary, holding place to stay before the final judgment day. Now, for the true Christians, their spirits will immediately go to paradise. But the spirits of the purposely-sinning people will immediately go to a hot hell to wait for the final judgment day. And after the final judgment, these same people will then be sent to the lake of fire. Here are the verses:

"Just as man is appointed to die once, and after this, the judgment."
- Hebrews 9:27

"The wicked shall be turned into hell, and all the nations that forget God."
- Psalm 9:17

And here is the final destination for the people who are purposely-sinning or immoral:

*"And whosoever was not found written in the **book of life** was cast into the **lake of fire**."* - Revelation 20:15

So, you can see that no one can escape GOD or beat Him. There is nothing called 'die and disappear to the thin air.' That belief is the utmost self-deception and a grave trickery from the devil to lead people to hell fire because he, himself is going there. And the devil wants as many people as he can get to go with him to fire.

Also, why is GOD referred to as the ALMIGHTY? One of the reasons is, you cannot escape His punishment when you purposely disregard His laws in your life. That is why JESUS describes purposely-sinning people as *"they do not know what they do."* (Luke 23:34)

Here then is the practical way you love GOD back:

✓ <u>You must obey His commandments, starting from the 10 commandments.</u> Here they are:

The Ten Commandments:

a. You shall have no other gods before me.

b. "You shall not make for yourself an image (idols) in the form of anything in heaven above or on the earth beneath or in the waters below. You shall not bow down to them or worship them.

c. You shall not take the name of the Lord your GOD in vain.

d. Keep the Sabbath day holy. (**Note**: What this means is that you must give rest to your body; and any day of the week is good to do so.) Here is what JESUS said when He worked to heal on the Jewish Sabbath day: *"Then he said to them, "The Sabbath was made for man, not man for the Sabbath."* (Mark 2:27)

e. Honor your father and your mother.

f. You shall not murder.

g. You shall not commit adultery.

h. You shall not steal.

i. You shall not bear false witness against your neighbor.

j. You shall not covet (envy, crave, lust after, yearn for) anything that belongs to your neighbor.
    - Exodus 20:1-17

And here are some of the works of the flesh (sins) that He wants you to run from:

"But if you are led by the Spirit, you are not under the law. The acts of the flesh are obvious: sexual immorality, impurity, and debauchery; idolatry and sorcery; hatred, discord, jealousy, and rage; rivalries, divisions, factions, and envy; drunkenness, orgies, and the like. I

warn you, as I did before, that those who practice such things will not inherit the kingdom of God." - Galatians 5:18-21

And please look at the sentence above that says *"But if you are led by the Spirit, you are not under the law."* That sentence begs for explanation. Why? It is because the evil-loving, Christians-in-name-only usually use that sentence to cover up their evil ways.

The verse says *if you are led by the Spirit,* it is then you are not under the law. **When you are led by the Spirit of GOD,** that means you are no longer doing things or living life according to your own feelings or according to the evil ways the world is doing things or the immoral ways your friends are doing things. Rather, you are now doing things according to how JESUS said they should be done.

But when GOD and JESUS are not the Ones dictating how you behave, how you think, and how you talk, then, **you are still under the law**, and you are bound to continue to sin because you cannot help yourself from sinning. Why? It is because sin is enticing and enjoyable for a moment; and it is the easiest way in life. In other words, without

JESUS, you will be compelled to do the acts of the flesh, which are sexual immorality, impurity, and debauchery (indecency, corruption perversion); idolatry, sorcery; hatred, discord, jealousy, rage; rivalries, divisions, factions, envy, drunkenness, orgies, and so on.

$$* * *$$

Well now, you might ask: "Is loving GOD back and loving people back a reciprocal thing?" 'Reciprocity' is not the right word. The correct words are <u>righteousness</u> and <u>justice</u>. All relationships come with responsibilities – written or unwritten. But there are relationships that are obviously based on written contracts. People know that a contract is a legally binding agreement that defines the rights and duties between/among parties. Two of the major contractual relationships are:

1. Marital relationship. This relationship is based on a contract where you vow and sign on to it. Therefore, the actions and words in this relationship should spring from (1) righteousness (doing what is right to the other partner), and (2) doing what is in the contract.

2. Relationship with GOD. A true

relationship with GOD is based on a contract. GOD is a contractual being.

Here is the thing - when you agree to be His child, that means you are agreeing to live by what He says; and He too will do what He promised. His side of the contract is, He promised to bless, protect, heal, prosper you, and at the end, He will allow you to enter His residence, heaven.

GOD'S actions towards you spring from (1) righteousness (He, doing what is right to you), and (2) He, doing what is written in the contract He too signed. See below what GOD does regarding the contract He signs with His true children:

"Then the LORD said to me, "You have seen well, for I am watching over My word to perform it." - Jeremiah 1:12

Absolutely, GOD watches over His promises to you to make sure He performs them.

Now, you may need to ask yourself this question if you are married, and that is, "Am I watching over my vow to my spouse to perform it?"

Also, if you say you are a Christian, you may need to ask yourself this, "Am I watching over my daily actions and words to make sure I play my part in the contract I signed with GOD?"

And, in case you do not know, see below the contract GOD signed with the children of Israel which He also signs with you personally when you decide to become His true child:

The contract with GOD

"If you fully obey the LORD your God and carefully follow all his commands I give you today, the LORD your God will set you high above all the nations on earth." - Deuteronomy 28:1

" However, if you do not obey the LORD your God and do not carefully follow all his commands and decrees I am giving you today, all these curses will come upon you and overtake you." - Deuteronomy 28:15

And here is what the children of Israel told GOD when signing the contract:

"And the people said to Joshua, "The LORD our God will we serve, and his voice will we obey."   - Joshua 24:24

But did they follow what was in the contract? No. And did they pay for breaking the condition in the contract? Yes. Greatly! Here is just one of their punishments:

"I scattered them with a whirlwind among all the nations, where they were strangers. The land they left behind them was so desolate that no one traveled through it. - Zechariah 7:14

The point is, when you are in a contract with GOD, He will fulfill His part of the contract, but when you fail to do your part, then GOD will cancel the contract. Here is what He said:

"If it (the country*) does evil in My sight and does not listen to My voice, then I will relent of the good I had intended for it."* - Jeremiah 18:10

And here is how GOD behaves:

"... The LORD is with you when you are with him. If you seek him, he will be found by you, <u>but if you forsake him, he will forsake you</u>."
- 2 Chronicles 15:2

Reader, you can see why lots of people go to hell, right? GOD is in a general contract with every person on earth, whether they know it or not; and He is in a special contract with His true children. The people who go to hell are those who refuse to fulfill their parts of the general contract when they forsake GOD as you saw above. And when you reject GOD, He will reject you.

<u>Therefore, when someone is doing what is right to you from LOVE, you need to do what is right to him/her from LOVE also.</u> You cannot just be on the receiving end, which is what a lot of people want.

And as you read above, <u>nobody can LOVE without GOD and JESUS</u>. Now, you may ask, "What about the people who lived before JESUS came to earth?" Good question! Those people were judged by GOD according to how they applied their conscience. Everyone is born with a conscience. But after JESUS came to earth, and you have had the opportunity to hear His message, then, you will now be judged by GOD/JESUS' commandments, and you will also be saved **only** through JESUS. Here are the verses:

"This Jesus is 'the stone you builders rejected, which has become the Chief cornerstone.' Salvation is found in no one else, for there is no other name under heaven given to mankind by which we must be saved." - Acts 4:11-12

"I am the vine, you are the branches. He who abides in Me, and I in him, bears much fruit; for without Me you can do nothing." - John 15:5

Indeed, it is when you are converted to JESUS that you can love GOD, JESUS, and people. Otherwise, you will continue to be good accidentally and occasionally, acting from culture, or you will be acting nice sometimes for a hidden, personal benefit. For example, here is how some parents show love to their children from a hidden, self-centered intention, and that is, they would do everything they can to help their children succeed in education and career with the hopes that these children would help them financially in future. But that is not how a godly person thinks. A person of GOD would help his/her children get good education and career to make sure his/her children do not suffer financially in life.

Definitely, without JESUS, your acts of kindness is never predictable or stable. An unstable person can be kind today, but comes tomorrow, he/she can be blatantly unhelpful and cruel. Why is that? It is because they cannot help themselves from being immoral. That is why Apostle Paul said the following in describing a human nature that is without GOD and JESUS:

"We know that the law is spiritual; but I am unspiritual, sold as a slave to sin."
- Romans 7:14

"For I do not do the good I want to do, but the evil I do not want to do—this I keep on doing."
- Romans 7:19

GOD and JESUS are the only ones that can bring moral stability into a person. This is why JESUS said *"No man is good, except GOD."* (Mark 10:18). And so, the very day you decide to truly start to obey GOD'S commandments, GOD and JESUS CHRIST will come to live in you, and they will start to be your driving force. They will start to live through you. In other words, how they say you should say things, that's how you say them; how they say you should do things, that's how you do them. Here is the verse:

"I have been crucified with Christ and I no longer live, but Christ lives in me. The life I now live in the body, I live by faith in the Son of God, who loved me and gave himself for me."
- Galatians 2:20

Hence, if you want the relationship between you and GOD or between you and another person to work out for peace and happiness, you must fulfill your obligations in the relationship, whether they are convenient to do or not.

So then, what is the meaning of LOVE?

- ✓ Love means you do things for someone else when it is not convenient for you to do so.
- ✓ Love means the words that come out of your mouth uplift people and not tear them down.
- ✓ Love means you do not put burdens on others that you cannot bear.
- ✓ Love means you feel the pains of the other person, or you put yourself in another person's shoes.
- ✓ Love is partly conditional and partly unconditional. Conditional means you have to work or do things for the other person to earn benefits from them.

IMPORTANT NOTE – Please know that only one person in a relationship CANNOT make a relationship to survive or blossom.

The two people in it must make efforts to fulfill their obligations in the union if there is going to be happiness between them. For example, if one person in a marriage relationship is fulfilling his/her obligations, and the other partner does not care, then, that union is bound to fail because there is going to be prevailing unfairness and conflict between them. Similarly, <u>GOD cannot carry on a one-sided relationship with you when you are the only one receiving the benefits while He gets zero</u>.

But you may say "there are couples who do not follow GOD and JESUS, and yet they appear to be happy together. No!!! It does not work that way! If you see couples that have married for a long time and they appear to be happy together without JESUS leading them, then they are living in one of the following conditions – 1) They are faking the appearance of happiness, 2) One of the partners is suffering silently to keep the other person happy, and 3) Both of them are struggling or managing to keep the marriage going. That's it! Many people suffer silently on earth. The partner who is quietly suffering usually is the one who lacks the following:

- Money, and

- A place to reside

People usually say "He that makes the gold makes the rules." You see that saying at play more in marriages. Absolutely, what makes a suffering spouse stay with a self-centered and an inconsiderate spouse are usually lack of money and a place to stay, or because of some other edges the spouse has over the sufferer.

Therefore, do not be fooled by the romantic words they express towards one another in the presence of people or their public display of affection. The bottom line is, any relationship where GOD and JESUS are not in both partners, the people in it are just managing to survive.

Also, in a marriage where one of the partners is exerting his/her edge over the other person, the one with the weapon usually determines when the sufferer can be happy or not. If the boss is not happy, he/she will make sure you too are not happy in one way or the other. Isn't that what the devil does? The devil is hurting today. That is why he moves around everywhere looking for the people he can hurt. Here is the verse:

"Be alert and of sober mind. Your enemy the devil prowls around like a roaring

lion looking for someone to devour."
- 1 Peter 5:8

And since the devil is not happy, this is the reason the people who are being used by him are not happy too. These people are ready to hurt someone in words and in deeds. There is a saying that "hurting people hurt people." You may be experiencing someone like that right now in your family or somewhere else.

Reader, all in all, if one is going to understand LOVE, one needs to understand how man was created. When you know how man was created, then it is easy to understand how love works. Therefore, let's quickly see the reality of the created man:

CHAPTER 6

Reality of Being Created as a Human

It is amazing to see that lots of people are not grateful for being created as humans instead of being created as animals. When GOD created the animals, He did not put His breath in them. But when He created man, He put His breath in him. Sure, animals are mobile, but they do not have GOD'S own breath.

Also, with regards to bodily form, man looks like GOD; but animals do not look like Him. See it here below:

"So God created mankind in his own image, in the image of God he created them; male and female he created them." - Genesis 1:27

Reader, is that not a great honor for you and Yours-truly that GOD created everybody in His image? GOD could have created man far less than Him, but He didn't. Is that LOVE from GOD or what?

But lots of people take that fact for granted and ignore the CREATOR and start to worship the created. Lucifer (now the devil), idols (molded images, carved images, fellow humans, animals) **were all created**. It is a fallen, degraded mind to leave the CREATOR and start to worship created things.

When GOD honored you by creating you in His image, you should honor Him back because He worked for that honor. GOD earned His honor and the love He desires back from you.

The LOVE for GOD is not forced or imposed. But realize that GOD spent part of His time to create everything one sees and enjoys on earth. He deserves a reward!

✳ ✳ ✳

So, here is the summation of LOVE according to how the CREATOR, GOD, set it up:

Summation of **LOVE**

1. *" Love the Lord your God with all your heart and with all your soul and with all your mind.'*

AND

2. *'Love your neighbor as you love yourself."*
- Matthew 22: 37-38

And below is what JESUS is telling you and Yours-truly today:

```
┌─────────────────────────────────────┐
│                                      │
│   LOVE  is  ( DO )                   │
│                                      │
│          Not empty talk.             │
│                                      │
└─────────────────────────────────────┘
```

"Do not merely listen to the word, and so deceive yourselves. Do what it says."
- James 1:22

Moreover, as you read above with regards to how man was created, the spirit that GOD put in you will never die because spirits do not die. The body dies but your spirit lives on. Therefore, it is the utmost mistake for anyone to think he/she can escape GOD'S punishments after choosing to continuously, willfully do wrongs to GOD and to people.

And since GOD put your spirit in you, He has the power and right to do whatever He wants with that spirit. GOD has the power to kill and the power to send anyone to hell, and with no opposition from anywhere. Here is what JESUS said about Him:

"But I will show you whom you should fear: Fear him who, after your body has been killed, has authority to throw you into hell. Yes, I tell you, fear him."
- Luke 12:5

Absolutely, your spirit will not die but will continue to live. The question is, which place will your spirit be when you leave the earth? This is the greatest question to ask oneself today.

And there are only two places for spirits to reside after physical death, and they are heaven or hell.

So, knowing that fact, the next question is, what criteria does GOD use to determine who goes to heaven and who goes to hell? Again, here comes the CONDITIONAL LOVE OF GOD.

> # With GOD, you have to earn your ENTRANCE to His heaven because admission into it is not free!

Let's repeat that – With GOD, you have to earn the ENTRANCE to heaven. You must work for it. GOD has requirement to be met by you in order to enter heaven. There is a price you have to pay for the entrance, and the price is <u>right-doing (righteousness)</u>, plus the <u>TRUST of GOD</u>.

Reader, you can see why people who rely only on GOD'S unconditional love end up in hell. See below what JESUS said will happen to Christians-in-name-only on the judgment day:

*"Not everyone who says to Me, 'Lord, Lord,' will enter the kingdom of heaven, but only he who does the will of My Father in heaven. Many will say to Me on that day, 'Lord, Lord, did we not prophesy in Your name, and in Your name drive out demons and perform many miracles?' Then I will tell them plainly, 'I never knew you; depart from Me, you workers of **lawlessness**!'*
- Matthew 7:21-23

Simply put – **no obeying His laws, no heaven.**

So, just as it is with GOD, that is how it is with humans. In any relationship, there are certain benefits you just have to earn from the other person. And not willing to earn the benefits is the major reason there are lots of problems in marriage relationships and in other relationships.

✳ ✳ ✳

Reader, now that you know what GOD needs from you in order to qualify to enter heaven, the question is, how do you start on the road that leads to heaven? It is simple. Here it is –

First, turn your face to GOD and tell Him you have sinned in the past. Ask Him to please forgive you of all your past sins. Tell Him you are very sorry for committing them. Then, ask Him to please write your name in the LAMB'S BOOK OF LIFE. Tell Him to come into your heart to start to lead you by His word daily. Ask all of those in JESUS' name.

So now that you have repented of your past sins and have asked for forgiveness - guess what? GOD will immediately forgive you of all your past sins, be it small or great. And now, you are born again, and you are now a new person. Here is the verse:

"Therefore if any man be in Christ, he is a new creation: old things are passed

away; behold, all things are become new." - 2 Corinthians 5:17

Therefore, from now on, GOD and JESUS CHRIST will start you on a new page in life. That new page is called the <u>path of righteousness</u>. And from now on, you will continue to stay in that path of doing what is right to GOD and doing what is right to people, without going back to your old immoral ways. Now, JESUS will write your name in His Book. Here are the verses:

"And into the city will be brought the glory and honor of the nations. But nothing unclean will ever enter it, nor anyone who practices an abomination or a lie, but only those whose names are written in the Lamb's Book of Life."
- Revelation 21:27

"He leads me in the paths of righteousness For His name's sake."
- Psalm 23:3

And here is another good news for you - do you know you will be celebrated in heaven on the very day you accept JESUS into your life? Surely, GOD, JESUS, and the host of heaven will celebrate your conversion. There will be joy in heaven. Here is the verse:

"I say to you that in the same way there will be joy in heaven over one sinner who repents…" - Luke 15:7

Actually, below is the illustration of your celebration on the day you choose GOD and JESUS over the devil:

"Jesus continued: "There was a man who had two sons. The younger one said to his father, 'Father, give me my share

of the estate.' So he divided his property between them. "Not long after that, the younger son got together all he had, set off for a distant country and there squandered his wealth in wild living. After he had spent everything, there was a severe famine in that whole country, and he began to be in need. So he went and hired himself out to a citizen of that country, who sent him to his fields to feed pigs. He longed to fill his stomach with the pods that the pigs were eating, but no one gave him anything. "When he came to his senses, he said, 'How many of my father's hired servants have food to spare, and here I am starving to death! I will set out and go back to my father and say to him: Father, I have sinned against heaven and against you. I am no longer worthy to be called your son; make me like one of your hired servants.' So he got up and went to his father. "But while he was still a long way off, his father saw him and was filled with compassion for him; he ran to his son, threw his arms around him and kissed him. "The son said to him, 'Father, I have sinned against heaven and against you. I am no longer worthy to be called your son.' "But the father said to his servants, 'Quick! Bring the best robe and put it on him. Put a ring on his finger and sandals on his feet. Bring the fattened calf and kill it. Let's have a feast and celebrate. For this son of mine was dead and is alive again; he was lost and is found.' So they began to celebrate. - Luke 15:11-24

And as a matter of fact, what you just read shows how valuable you are to GOD. He highly regards you when you become His child in this evil world.

And do you know there is a definition of who is a child of GOD? Surely, there is! Why is this important for you to know? It is because lots of people claim they are children of GOD when they are not. Therefore, see below the definition of who is a child of GOD:

"For those who are led by the Spirit of God are the children of God."
- Romans 8:14

✳ ✳ ✳

Therefore, now that you are born again, it is time for you to actually know GOD, JESUS, and the HOLY SPIRIT, and how the Kingdom of GOD works. Typically, before people become born again, they have preconceived ideas about who GOD and JESUS are. And these preconceived notions are based on what they hear from people and from Preachers. But if you base your beliefs about GOD and JESUS only on what you hear from people, you will not understand GOD. That is why it is crucial you get a copy of the Bible and start reading it from cover to cover. Why do you have to do this? It is because there are numerous things about GOD and JESUS in the Bible that Preachers and other people will never tell you. But you need these information to understand GOD and JESUS. In fact, here is what GOD said about you reading the Bible for yourself:

"Study to show yourself approved unto God, a workman that needs not to be ashamed, rightly dividing the word of truth." - 2 Timothy 2:15

Then, after that, the next thing to do is to belong to a church or a Bible study group that actually teaches how to stay away from sins. You need to run from 'religious churches' that are ritual-based, or prosperity-centered, instead of teaching GOD'S laws. Prosperity-based churches focus on how to use faith to obtain prosperity, healing, and protection from GOD. These types of churches are **things seekers**. Their leaders do not care about your soul. They only want your tithes and offerings. They are eloquent in identifying your problems, but after that, they give you feel-good sermons that cannot solve your problems.

Then the ritual-based churches are the ones that are into observances, performing outward religious procedures or religious actions in customary ways that have nothing to do with changing man's heart for good. In these types of churches, their leaders take you through outward religious activities in the service to condition you to think you are a Christian. Then after the service, you go home still being immoral as you were before you went there. Run from such churches because they are not teaching you what will help you become moral or right-minded.

Also, if you are attending a church that is constantly feeding you feel-good sermons from Sunday to Sunday, telling you how God is going to bless you, protect you, and heal you, without telling you GOD'S CONDITION for getting those things, run from them. They make you feel good for few minutes while you are listening to them, but they are actually weakening you spiritually. They are feeding you milk to keep you down and prevent you from having any spiritual power and freedom. Here is what Apostle Paul said about that:

"Although by this time you ought to be teachers, you need someone to reteach

you the basic principles of God's word. You need milk, not solid food! For everyone who lives on milk is still an infant, inexperienced in the <u>message of righteousness</u>. But solid food is for the mature, who by constant use have trained their senses to distinguish <u>good from evil.</u> " - Hebrews 5:12-14

GOD and JESUS want you to eat solid food; that is, to be hearing messages on how to be holy like GOD, instead of constantly feeding on "how God will bless you," "how God will protect you," and "how God will heal you" messages.

Do not let these types of Pastors, Preachers, and Prophets fool you. GOD will bless, protect, and heal you when you commit to doing what is right to GOD and doing what is right to people, starting from your home.

<u>Protection, healing, and other blessings come with the package of **righteousness** and **trust** of GOD. GOD will add them to you.</u> Here is the verse:

"But seek first the kingdom of God and His righteousness, and all these things shall be added to you." - Matthew 6:33

Also, run from fake Prophets who say you are going to get miracles this week, this month, etc. but will not tell you how to stay away from sins, which is the condition GOD requires in order for you to get His miraculous blessings.

Certainly, real Prophets are highly needed in a society because they speak the mind of GOD. But do not be fooled by fake ones. See below what GOD said about the fake ones:

"This is what the LORD of Hosts says: "Do not listen to the words of the prophets who prophesy to you. They are filling you with false hopes. They speak visions from their own minds, not from the mouth of the LORD. They keep saying to those who despise Me, 'The LORD says that you will have peace,'

and to everyone who walks in the stubbornness of his own heart, 'No harm will come to you.' But which of them has stood in the council of the LORD to see and hear His word? Who has given heed to His word and obeyed it?"
- Jeremiah 23:16-18

See below the job of a **true** Prophet:

"But if they had stood in My council, they would have proclaimed My words to My people and turned them back from their evil ways and deeds."
- Jeremiah 23:21-22

And here are the signs of a true Prophet:

1. Whatever he/she prophesied must come to pass, (Deuteronomy 18:22), and

2. They are to warn people to stop their immoral ways so they can avoid on-coming punishments from GOD.

The bottom line is:

You should only follow religious leaders who warn you of the consequences of sins so GOD can bless you and heal your land.

Now, here is the summation of actions that bloom LOVE in a relationship:

CHAPTER 7

What Blooms Love In A Relationship

If you are in a continuing relationship with someone, whether it is with GOD, your spouse, your father, mother, your children, siblings, friends, other relatives, etc. and you desire LOVE from them, then you need to do the following:

✓ **Start doing things** for the person when it is not convenient for you to do so. It is called work. Certainly, nobody likes work, but that is why you get paid for doing it or reap the benefits. But if you do not want to work to earn the love from the other person, <u>then, do not enter into relationship with the person. Also, do not say "I love GOD" when you are not ready to obey His commandments because GOD is not into words but into actions.</u>'

✓ **Consideration** - Be attentive, concerned, and mindful of the other person. If you want the other person to consider you when doing things or when making decisions, you must do the same to him/her. Consideration includes not putting burdens you cannot bear on the other person.

✓ <u>**Helping**</u> – If you want your partner to help you in different ways, you need to do the same to him/her

✓ <u>**Patience**</u> – If you want your partner to have patience towards you, then you need to be patient towards him/her.

✓ **<u>Kindness</u>** – If you want your partner to be intentionally doing good to you, then you need to do the same to him/her.

✓ **<u>Accommodating</u>** – If you want your partner to put up with you in certain areas of your life, then you need to do the same to him/her.

✓ **<u>Cooperation</u>** – If you want your partner to always be involved in assisting you to achieve your goals or common goals, then you need to assist him/her in achieving his/her goals.

✓ **<u>Unselfish</u>** – If you want your partner to be willing to put your needs and wishes above his/hers, then you need to do the same to him/her.

✓ **<u>Compassion</u>** – If you want your partner to feel your pains and to show sympathy, care, and concern when you are going through hard times, then you need to start doing the same towards him/her.

✓ **<u>Generosity</u>** - If you want your partner to be readily willing to give to you, then you need to start doing the same to him/her.

✓ **<u>Respect</u>** – If you want your partner to be polite, respectful, and well-mannered toward you, then you need to start doing the same to him/her.

Etc.

But if you are not a true Christian, you may look at that list above and say you can do them to your partner without GOD/JESUS living in you. Please know up-front that you are bound to fail. Why? It is because a natural man without GOD and JESUS is wicked. How do we know that? We know that because the manufacturer of humans said so, and your experiences of people confirm it.

There is a saying that the manufacturer of a product knows the product best. GOD is the manufacturer of humans. Does He not know humans best? See below how He described humans:

"The heart is deceitful above all things, and desperately wicked; Who can know it?" - Jeremiah 17:9

Marriage relationship, for example, is as healthy as the two people in it. It is only GOD/JESUS that can make the heart healthy, and no other way. So, when JESUS comes into your life, He will change your heart from being wicked/immoral and self-centered, to being moral by doing to others what you want done to you.

Reader, in closing, GOD and JESUS are beckoning to you today to come to them so you can start receiving the benefits in store for you, just like the Prodigal son in the parable you saw earlier.

The question now is, are you going to let JESUS become the MANAGER of your life from now on or not? Would you humble yourself today to ask Him for forgiveness and start to follow His ways, **so you can start to have everlasting happiness and peace?** Would you choose Him?

Also know that, for sure, when you choose JESUS, you will have nothing to lose, but you will have everything to gain. Taste and see that the LORD is good; blessed is the one who takes refuge in Him. (Psalm 34:8).

We pray that you do not harden your heart today, but listen to GOD and to His Son, JESUS, to choose Him, and reject the devil's ways. And all will be well with you forever.

Best Wishes.

OUR OTHER AVAILABLE BOOKS

1. *Christians Going To Heaven Christians Going To Hell*

---

2. *Relationship Should Be 50/50 If Not It Won't Work*

---

3. *Why Most Christians & Others Are Not Happy*

4. *Enviable Life of A True Christian*

www.ingramcontent.com/pod-product-compliance
Lightning Source LLC
Chambersburg PA
CBHW060945040426
42445CB00011B/1013